Contents

Me and my class

3. Using my journal.....................☐
4. Our Essential Agreements ....☐
6. My learner profile.....................☐
8. The learner profile in action............☐
10. Reflecting on my learner profile....☐
11. What action can I take? ....☐
12. What kind of learner am I? ....
13. Understanding my learning style ...☐
14. My classroom and learning space....☐
15. Reaching a goal.....................☐

Self-management skills

16. My basic needs ....☐
17. Sustainable Development Goals ......☐
20. Practising mindfulness ....☐
21. Practising being present..................☐
22. How to calm down ....☐
23. Being distracted.....................☐
24. Celebrating mistakes ....☐
25. Keep going!.....................☐
26. Never give up.....................☐
27. Checking in with myself.....................☐
28. Well-being checklist.....................☐
29. Task cards.....................☐

Communication skills

30. Understanding body language ....☐
31. What makes a good communicator?.....................☐
32. Practising listening skills...............☐
33. Practising speaking skills ....☐
34. Becoming a reflective reader and writer ....☐
35. Reflecting on learning.....................☐
36. Two smiles and a wish ....☐
37. Task cards ....☐

Social skills

38. Caring for others ....☐
39. Ways to help others ....☐
40. Helping others.....................☐
41. How can I help?.....................☐
42. Playing games with others ....☐
43. Working in a group.....................☐

Social skills

44. Managing my emotions in group work .... ☐
45. Roles in a group .... ☐
46. Reflecting on group work .... ☐
47. Task cards .... ☐

Thinking skills

48. Becoming a critical thinker .... ☐
49. Finding relationships and connections .... ☐
50. Making connections when reading .... ☐
51. Reflecting on units of inquiry .... ☐
54. Thinking deeply about a picture ...... ☐
56. Making decisions .... ☐
57. Taking action .... ☐
58. Becoming a creative thinker .... ☐
59. Using creative ideas .... ☐
60. Pros and cons .... ☐
61. Reflecting to help me make decisions .... ☐
62. Task cards .... ☐

Research skills

63. Thinking about questions .... ☐
64. Writing questions .... ☐
65. Finding answers to questions .... ☐
66. Sorting information .... ☐
67. Being a principled researcher .... ☐
68. Presenting information .... ☐
69. I wonder .... ☐
70. Task cards .... ☐

Reflection

71. Reflecting on my year .... ☐

Using my journal

Welcome

This is your journal. Please use it to draw or write your ideas and thoughts.

There are no right or wrong answers – be free to explore.

Reflection helps us to develop an awareness of ourselves and others.

Reflection can be …

Being aware of the present. Describing your feelings.

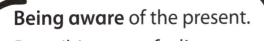

Wondering. Giving your point of view. Making connections.

Thinking back on your day. Thinking forward to how to improve.

Planning goals for yourself and next steps. Planning how to use your skills to take action.

3

Our Essential Agreements

Essential agreements help to keep the class safe and happy. They show how **caring** we can be.

What helps you to be a good learner?

What makes you feel safe and happy at school?

How can you help make other people feel happy in school?

4

What would you like to have in your essential agreements?

💬 Are your agreements the same as your classmates' agreements?
Are they different?

My learner profile

When do you show each of these learner profile attributes? Add your ideas.

Which learner profile attributes are you good at?
Which attributes would you like to develop?
How would you start to develop them?

The learner profile in action

Frida Kahlo lived in Mexico. When she was eighteen she had a bad accident. She had to stay in bed for a long time. She gave up her plan of becoming a doctor.

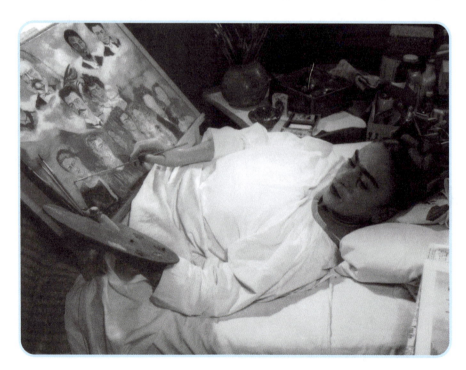

As she lay in bed, Frida started painting. She painted colourful pictures full of plants and animals. Her paintings were very different from other art of the time.

Frida was in pain all her life, but she loved to paint and spend time outside. She taught other people how to paint too.

What do you wonder about this story?

Which learner profile attributes did Frida show?

Did she show one more than others?

Reflecting on my learner profile

Create a learner profile castle!

1 Choose a colour for each attribute. Add them to the key below.

2 Colour in each part of the castle to match an attribute. Make the **tallest** parts of the castle the attributes you are **best** at.

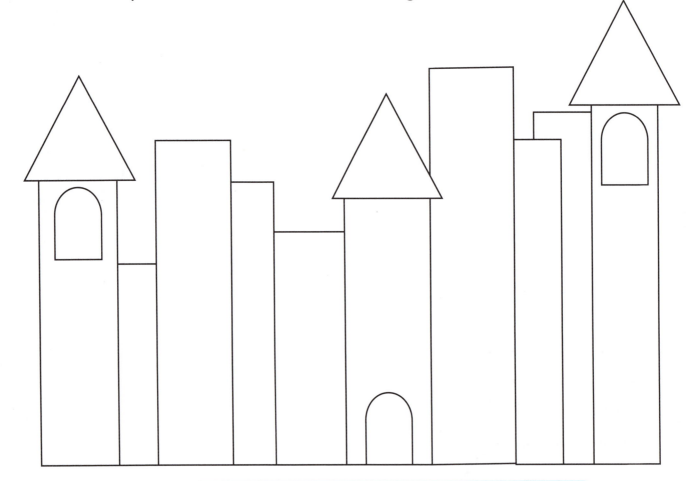

Attribute	Colour	Attribute	Colour
Thinker		Knowledgeable	
Inquirer		Risk-taker	
Caring		Open-minded	
Principled		Reflective	
Balanced		Communicator	

 Notice how your castle is different to your classmates' castles. What makes you unique?

What action can I take?

> You have a super power! If you are **principled** and a **risk-taker**, you can make the world a better place. You can take action. It can be as big or as small as you want.

Think about something you would like to change. Draw or write about it here.

What action might you take?

Action I can take myself	
Action my community can take 	

 Discuss your ideas with a partner. Do you have any similar ideas?

11

What kind of learner am I?

Understanding yourself as a learner helps you know how to learn best.

1 Colour the speech bubbles using this key.

- 🟩 I always remember
- 🟨 I sometimes remember
- 🟧 This can be a challenge

2 Ask your classmates which way they remember things best: by seeing, doing or hearing. Add a tally mark for each classmate in one of the boxes below. 𝍲

"I remember things from what I **see**."

"I remember things from what I **do**."

"I remember things from what I **hear**."

See

Do

Hear

12

Understanding my learning style

Do you remember best what you see, do or hear? Circle the picture that shows what type of learner you are.

Because of my learning style …

I like to …	I get distracted by …

💬 Find a partner with the same learning style as you.
Compare your tables and discuss connections.
What might stop you getting distracted?
Which learner profile attribute might help?

My classroom and learning space

Classrooms are important places where we become better communicators, work together, have fun and learn more about ourselves and the world around us.

What are your two favourite spaces in your classroom?
Draw and write about them.

I like this because ....
....
....
....
....

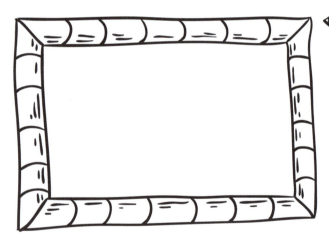

I like this because ....
....
....
....
....

 Think about how essential agreements are used in your classroom. Which essential agreement do you think is the most important?

....
....

 Discuss with a partner and compare.

14

Reaching a goal

Sometimes, setting a goal can be like climbing a mountain.
You need to break your goal into smaller steps.

1 Choose a goal that you would like to achieve this year.

My goal is to ....

....

2 I will reach my goal using these three small steps:

15

My basic needs

We all have basic needs. These are things we need to stay alive.

What are your basic needs? Make a list of them below.

Remember, these are things you need, not things you want.

Sustainable Development Goals

The world has 17 Sustainable Development Goals (SDGs). These goals aim to make the world a better place. Here are four of the goals.

Good health and well-being
Everyone should have access to healthy lifestyles and health services.

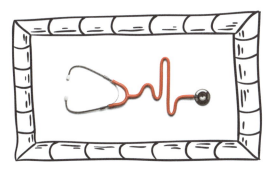

 What is important for a healthy lifestyle?

fruit and vegetables

Sustainable Development Goals

Quality education

We should all get to go to school and learn.

 Why is quality education important?

 ## Gender equality
Boys and girls should have the same rights and opportunities.
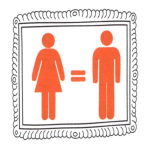 

 What opportunities are important for both boys and girls to have?

education

 ## Clean water and sanitation
We should all have access to clean water.

 What do you use water for? Write a list.

Practising mindfulness

Being mindful means living in the **now**. We can be **balanced** and practise this by using our senses. This means noticing what we hear, see, smell, taste and touch.

Look at this picture. What might you be able to hear, see, smell, taste or touch? Write or draw your ideas around the picture.

 Share your ideas with a partner.

Practising being present

Self-Management ✓

1 Close your eyes.

2 Use your sense of hearing to connect to the present.

3 What sounds can you hear?

What did you notice?

....

....

This was ...   😊 easy   🙁 difficult   because ....

....

How might using your senses help you learn?

21

How to calm down

Being present can help us calm down when we are stressed or worried. We can be present by being **thinkers** and connecting to our senses.

Stop what you are doing. Notice what you can see, hear and feel.

3 things I see …

2 things I hear …

1 thing I feel …

Share and compare with a partner.

Being distracted

What are some ways you can stop yourself being distracted?

When I am distracted, I can …

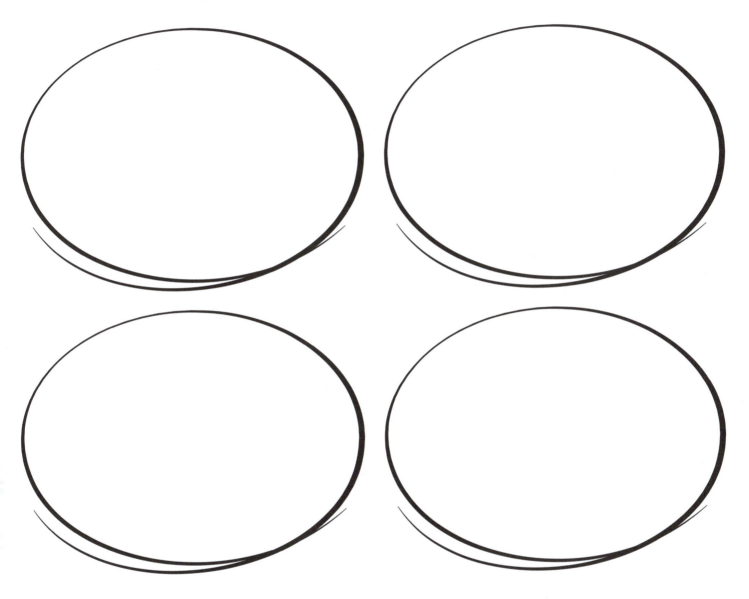

Managing distractions will help me ....

....

....

 How can you help others to manage their distractions?

23

Celebrating mistakes

Instead of feeling bad when you make mistakes, be **reflective**. Mistakes are ways we can learn to be better.

Lots of things have been invented from people making mistakes!

Sticky notes

A scientist was trying to make a strong glue. But he only made a weak glue. He thought he had failed.

Years later, another scientist wanted a bookmark that wouldn't fall out. He knew the weak glue wouldn't leave sticky marks on the pages. He used the weak glue to stick his bookmark in.

Sticky notes were invented!

When have you made a mistake? What did you learn?

 Share your story with a partner.

Keep going!

A growth mindset means that you learn from mistakes and don't give up.
A fixed mindset stops you getting better at things.

Colour the statements below.
Use **red** for a **fixed** mindset. Use **green** for a **growth** mindset.

| I can't do this! | I can learn from mistakes. | I give up! |

| Mistakes are how I learn. | This might take some time to learn. | This is not going to work. |

| I'll try it a different way. | I tried and it didn't work. | I will ask for help with this. |

Can you think of some of your own?
Write them here, then colour them in.

 Share and compare your statements with a partner.

25

Never give up

Be a **risk-taker** and keep going, even when it feels hard, or even impossible. This is how we succeed!

Look at this picture of 'The Learning Pit'. What might the boy be thinking at each stage? Add thought bubbles.

 Have you ever felt like you were in the Learning Pit? How did you succeed?

 Share your story with a partner.

Checking in with myself

Being **balanced** means being mindful of your emotions and well-being every day.

Complete the well-being checklist.

Today, I feel …

Do I need to talk to an adult about anything?   Yes ☐   No ☐

My energy level is … (circle one)

very low   low   ok   good   great!

Why could this be?

   Talk to a partner. How will you look after your well-being today?

Well-being checklist

Make your own well-being checklist for yourself or others to use. What is important to you?

Task cards

Role-playing situations is a great way to be **reflective**, good **thinkers** and strong **communicators**. You can find ways to solve problems.

Read these task cards and act them out.

As a class, discuss the situations and find solutions.

You did not sleep well last night and you feel tired and grumpy. Your friend is excited about coming to your house later and is asking you lots of questions.

What could you do?

You are trying to work at school but other students at your table are talking and distracting you.

What could you do?

You have been given a task that you find very difficult. You are feeling frustrated and want to give up.

What could you do?

You have a friend at school who gives up on everything. They use negative talk such as "I will never understand this!" and "I give up!"

What could you do?

Write your own task cards below.

Understanding body language

We can be good **communicators** by using our bodies to show ideas and thoughts to others.

Mime artists tell stories using only actions. They do not speak.
What might these actions mean?

What might these expressions mean?

 Work with a partner or group to make up a story only using actions. Perform it for your classmates.

What makes a good communicator?

To be a good **communicator**, it is important to be a good listener and speaker.

What do good speakers and listeners do?

A good listener …

A good speaker …

Practising listening skills

Which picture is the odd one out? Why?

Partner game

1. Think of three connected objects. Now think of an object which isn't connected to the others. For example: apple, pear, car, grapes.

2. Say these objects to a partner.
   Let your partner guess which the odd one out is.

3. Remind them to explain why it is the odd one out.

Class game

Play the game 'I went shopping and I bought …'

… I bought apples.

… I bought apples and bananas.

… I bought apples, bananas and cake.

 How did you remember everything?
Could you use this to remember other things?

32

Practising speaking skills

1 Hide something in a box. Describe it to your partner without saying what it is. Can they guess the object?

This was … easy difficult because ....

....

....

2 Tell a partner how to tie their shoelaces **without** showing them!

This was … easy difficult because ....

....

33

Becoming a reflective reader and writer

Read something that is linked to your unit of inquiry.
Use the Think/Puzzle/Explore table to reflect on it further.

Think 💡 What do you think you know about this topic?	
Puzzle 🧩 What questions do you have?	
Explore 🔍 What do you want to explore further?	

 Share your thoughts with a partner. Compare and discuss.

 Where can you find out more?

Other...

Reflecting on learning

Be **reflective**, then share your thoughts with others. This will help you to become a better **communicator**.

Use these sentence starters to help you reflect on your day or week.

I can help myself by

I'd like to be more

I'm looking forward to

 Share with a partner. Were any of your reflections similar to theirs? What other sentence starters could you use?

Two smiles and a wish

 Use 'Two smiles and a wish' to give feedback.

The smiles are two things you think someone has done well.

 The wish is something you think they could improve.

Look at your partner's work.

Write some feedback using sentence starters like these:

I really like …   I noticed …   I learned …   You could try …

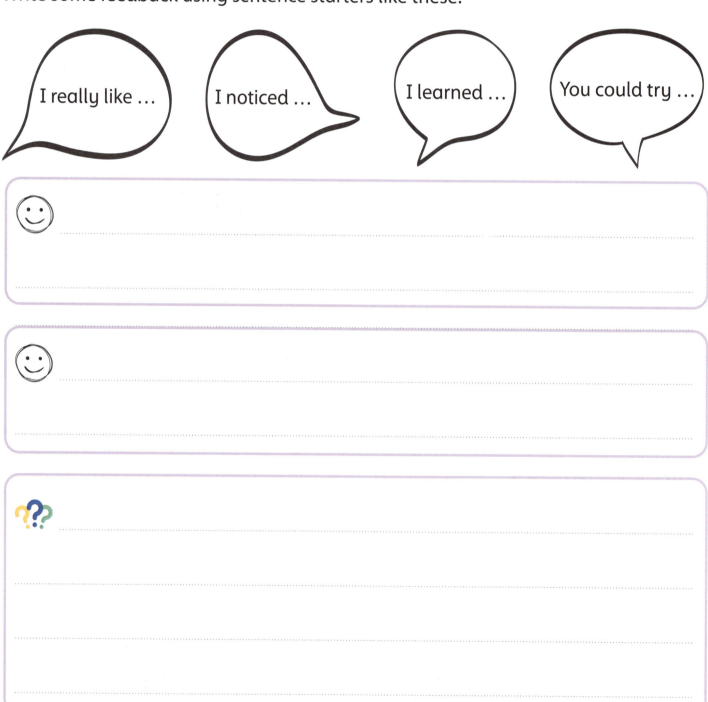

Task cards

Communication

Role-play is a great way to be **reflective**, good **thinkers** and strong **communicators**. You can find ways to solve problems.

Read these task cards and act them out.
As a class, discuss the situations and find solutions.

You notice that one of your friends is very quiet. You can tell that something is wrong.

What could you do?

You have forgotten to bring your homework into school. You are worried your teacher will be angry.

What could you do?

Your group has been asked to sing a song. You do not enjoy singing and do not think you have a good voice. You want to tell your group how you are feeling.

What could you do?

Your teacher has asked everyone to share a piece of research. Your friend is nervous and scared to speak in front of the class.

What could you do?

Write your own task cards below.

37

Caring for others

Noticing other people's reactions and emotions helps you to become more **caring**.

Look at this picture.
What do you see, think and wonder?

I see that

I think that

I wonder

How could you help others who are upset?

Ways to help others

What do you need when you are upset? Would it be the same for others? Write or draw ways that you can help others when they are upset.

 Discuss with a partner. What was similar or different about your answers?

39

Helping others

When you see someone upset and needing help, what do you do? How can you be **caring** and show that you want to help?

Think of a time when you helped someone. Draw it below.

What happened?

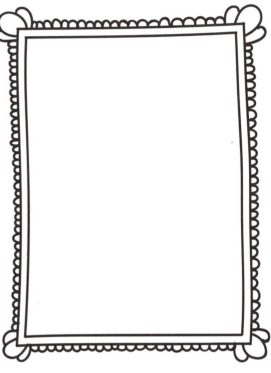

How did you help?

How did you feel about helping?

 Think about a time when someone helped you.
How do you think they felt after they helped you? Why?

40

How can I help?

We can help others in many places that we go. From teachers or friends, to our families or strangers, there is always someone who needs help.

Think of some times when you might be able to help others.

At school …

At home …

In your local community …

I'll do this today …

Tell a partner about your plan to help someone. Which SDG does it link to?

41

Playing games with others

> Playing games can be a lot of fun. Sometimes there can be conflict, though. Be **reflective**. How do you react when there is conflict?

Decide on a game to play in a group.

While you play, be mindful of your words, actions and feelings.

Write your thoughts below.

I played the game ....

I used …	I felt …
I tried …	I wondered …

I learned …

Working in a group

People who work well in groups are **open-minded**, **caring** and good **communicators**.

What do you like and dislike about working in groups?

What I like about group work	What I find difficult about group work

 Which learner profile attributes do you use when you work in a group?

43

Managing my emotions in group work

Conflict can happen when you are working in a group. Be **balanced** and learn some ways of managing your emotions when this happens.

How can you keep calm when you are upset?
Draw or write your ideas.

I can take big, deep breaths.

Share your ideas with a partner.
Add more ideas if your partner has different suggestions.

Roles in a group

> Giving people a role (job) can help everyone work better together.

During a group activity, agree who will do these roles. Write their names in the boxes.

Facilitator
They lead the group. They make sure the group stays focused and that everyone's ideas are heard.

Time keeper
They make sure the group will finish on time.

Recorder
They write down what is discussed.

Reporter
They tell the class about the group's project.

I was the ....

I felt ....

....

The learner profile attribute I used the most was ....

45

Reflecting on group work

> Being **reflective** helps you to see what worked and what didn't work. This means you can make positive changes in the future.

Reflect on your group work.
Put a tick in the box that fits the best.

	🙂	😐	☹
Everyone was given a role.			
Everyone was focused during the activity.			
All ideas were listened to and respected.			
The activity was completed on time.			
The group worked well and had fun.			

I learned ....

....

Next time, I can ....

....

Task cards

Role-playing situations is a great way to be **reflective**, good **thinkers** and strong **communicators**. You can find ways to solve problems.

Read these task cards and act them out.

As a class, discuss the situations and find solutions.

You see someone that you don't know very well fall over and hurt themselves. They are crying and can't get up.

What could you do?

There's a new child in your class. At breaktime, you notice that they are by themselves.

What could you do?

You are working in a group to create a new game. Everyone is arguing and getting upset.

What could you do?

You have an argument with a close friend. You feel very sad and upset. They are very angry and don't want to talk to you.

What could you do?

Write your own task cards below.

47

Becoming a critical thinker

Being a critical thinker means you try to see things from both sides. This helps you to become **open-minded**.

Look at the picture below. Write a speech bubble for each child.

How could this conflict be resolved?

 Why is it important to see situations from both sides?

Finding relationships and connections

(Critical **thinkers** find relationships and connections between things.)

What connections can you find between these objects?

Explain your ideas about how these things are connected.

....

....

....

....

 Compare your ideas with a partner.
Which ideas are similar and which are different? Why might this be?

Making connections when reading

Think about a book you know. What connections can you make?

Name of book:

This reminds me of a time I …

This reminds me of something else I read. It was about …

This character reminds me of …

I would/would not recommend this book because

Reflecting on units of inquiry

Being **reflective** about your units of inquiry can help you become more **knowledgeable** and take action.

Reflect on each unit of inquiry from the year.

Think about what you learned and why this might be helpful to you.

What I learned … • This will help me to …

- Who we are
- Where we are in place and time
- How we express ourselves

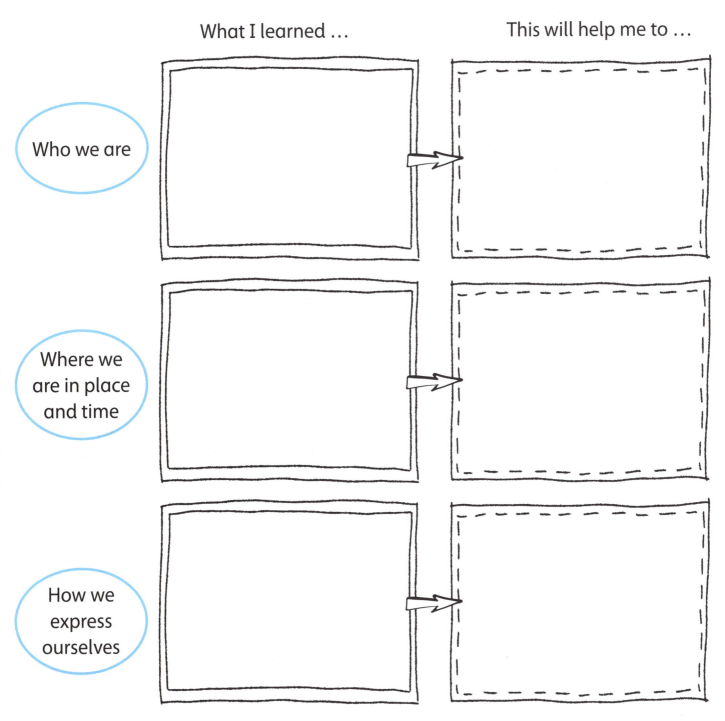

51

Reflecting on units of inquiry

What I learned …   This will help me to …

- How the world works
- Sharing the planet
- How we organize ourselves

Which unit of inquiry did you enjoy most?

....

Reflect on why you liked it. Use the ideas below to help you.

Being
Have you changed how you behave? Are you kinder or more patient?

Feeling
Do you feel different? Were you worried about anything, or were you confident?

Doing
Did you do something? Did you help someone or make something?

Having
Do you have more of something? Knowledge? Respect? Determination?

Thinking
Have you thought in a different way? Did you change your mind? Did you wonder or inquire?

Saying
What did you say? How did you say it? Did you discuss, explain or debate?

 What action did you take after the unit? Which SDG did it link to?

53

Thinking deeply about a picture

> Looking at things carefully helps you to be **knowledgeable**.
> Be **inquirers**. Ask interesting questions and use what you already know.

Look at these pictures and think about the questions.

What can you see?

How are these objects normally used?

Who uses them?

Why have they been left?

Write your ideas here:

 Share your notes with a partner.

Sometimes you might only see part of the 'bigger picture'. Being a **thinker** and considering what is important helps to organize your thoughts.

Look at the whole picture, then answer these questions.

What can you see?

When was this picture taken?

Who is in the picture?

Where was this picture taken?

Why are they there?

💬 Share your thoughts with a partner.

55

Making decisions

> Make decisions by using what you see, think and feel. Remember to be **principled**. This will help you to decide if action needs to be taken.

Answer the questions to decide if action should be taken or not.

What action can be taken?

Who will take action?

Where will the action take place?

When will the action take place?

Why should action be taken?

....
....
....
....
....
....
....

💬 Share your thoughts with a partner.

# Taking action

There are many ways to take action. You might need to be a **risk-taker** and try something new!

Fixing the problem of litter might include taking action and helping others.
Or it might include changing the way you live.

 Decide on an action plan. Write your ideas below.
Share with your class. See if this action can become a class project.

How successful were you?
Circle the face that shows how you did.

 What would you change if you did it again?
How does your action link to these goals?

57

Becoming a creative thinker

New inventions and ideas come from people who are **risk-takers** and creative **thinkers**.

What if you could invent a machine to help someone you know?

It could be a parent/carer or teacher.
It might help them at home, or help them do their job.
Use this space to help organize your ideas.

Share your thoughts with a partner.

Using creative ideas

Choose one of your ideas. Draw pictures and make notes about it.

 Share your invention ideas with a partner.

Pros and cons

Think about the pros (good points) and cons (bad points) of your idea. This will help you to understand if it is a good idea or not.

Pros 🙂 | Cons ☹

My final decision. Will it work? Why?

Reflecting to help me make decisions

Reflecting on what you have done in the past helps you to make decisions in the future.

Use these questions to reflect on your learning.

What new thing did I learn?	What was I most proud of?
What would I do differently?	**What did I notice about my thinking?**

 Which learner profile attributes did you use during this activity?

Task cards

> Role-playing situations is a great way to be **reflective**, good **thinkers** and strong **communicators**. You can find ways to solve problems.

Read these task cards and act them out.
As a class, discuss the situations and find solutions.

You see someone throw a piece of litter on the floor.

What could you do?

You are working in a group. Everyone has very good ideas. You are not sure how to decide which idea to use.

What could you do?

Your friend wants to find out more about something. They don't know where to find the information.

What could you do?

It's your birthday. Your mum has not sent in enough cupcakes for each child in your class. She has sent two less than you need.

What could you do?

Write your own task cards below.

62

Thinking about questions

There are many ways to ask questions. These question words help us find out different types of information.

1. Look at the question words.
2. Which is the most useful word? Write it in the top box.
3. Write the other question words in order.

Most important

Least important

What?

Where?

How?

Why?

Who?

When?

💬 Share your order with a partner.
What do you notice?
What is the same or different about how you ordered the question words?
Why might this be?

63

Writing questions

Being an **inquirer** and asking questions about the world around you will help you to become more **knowledgeable**.

Cheetah cub

Axolotl

Elephant

Other

Choose a picture of one of the animals above or find a picture that you like. Think of some questions that you can ask to find out more.

 What?

 Where?

 How?

 Why?

 Who?

When?

Finding answers to questions

There are many places we can find answers to our questions (**sources**). The more sources you use, the more likely it is that you will find the right answer.

asking someone

Choose a question that you would like to answer.
Write it in the centre.
Add some sources where you could find an answer.

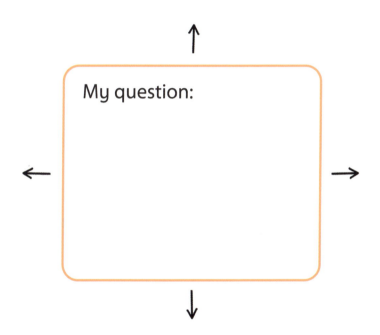

Circle the sources that you will use.
How does your question link to this goal?

65

Sorting information

Sometimes, it is difficult to know which information is important and what might not be needed. You can use the 3-2-1 strategy to organize your thoughts.

3 facts I learned …

2 new words I had not heard of before …

1 question I still have …

Being a principled researcher

Be **principled** and share information in your own words. Don't just copy it! It is also important to say where the information came from.

Write all the places where you found your information below:

Presenting information

Sharing your new knowledge helps others to become more **knowledgeable**. There are many ways you can present (show) what you found out.

Here are some ways you can present information.
Can you think of some other ways? Draw them in the spaces below.
Circle the way you would like to present your information.

Present what you wrote on page 66 to your class in your favourite way!

Reflect on the way you shared your information.
How well did you share what you knew?
Draw a circle around the face that fits best.

I wonder ...

It is great to be an **inquirer** and to wonder about things. Wanting to know more will help you to develop important skills that can make the world a better place.

What do you wonder about?

I wonder why ...

 Take some time to do your own research and share it with your class.
Create a 'Wonder wall' in your class with lots of different questions.

Task cards

Role-playing situations is a great way to be **reflective**, good **thinkers** and strong **communicators**. You can find ways to solve problems.

Read these task cards and act them out.

As a class, discuss the situations and find solutions.

You have been given a topic to research.

What sources would you use to find out information?

You have been asked to present your research to the class.

How will you present your research?

Your teacher has given your class a list of words that you don't understand.

How could you find out what the words mean?

You have been given a research task to complete with a partner. Your partner starts copying the information without changing it into their own words.

What could you do?

Write your own task cards below.

Reflecting on my year

Something I learned …

Something I am proud of …

The SDG I thought about the most was …

The learner profile attribute that I used the most was …

Reflecting on my year

The book I loved the most was about

A memory I'll keep

Next year, I hope to